WORLD OF ANIMALS

APES AND MONKEYS

BROWN
BEAR
BOOKS

Published by Brown Bear Books Limited

An imprint of
The Brown Reference Group plc
68 Topstone Road
Redding
Connecticut
06896
USA
www.brownreference.com

© 2008 The Brown Reference Group plc

This hardcover edition is distributed in the
United States by
Black Rabbit Books
P.O. Box 3263
Mankato, MN 56002

Library of Congress Cataloging-in-Publication Data
Hardyman, Robyn.
  Apes and monkeys / by Robyn Hardyman.
    p. cm. -- (The world of animals)
  Includes index.
  Summary: "Describes the behavior, physical
      characteristics, and habitats of different
      species of apes and monkeys"--Provided
      by publisher.
  ISBN-13: 978-1-933834-37-5
1. Apes--Juvenile literature. 2. Monkeys--
Juvenile literature. I. Title.
QL737.P96H3647 2009
599.8--dc22
                        2007049946

ISBN-13: 978-1-933834-37-5
ISBN-10: 1-933834-37-4

For the Brown Reference Group plc
Designer: Paul Myerscough
Editor: Sarah Eason
Creative Director: Jeni Child
Children's Publisher: Anne O'Daly
Editorial Director: Lindsey Lowe

Consultant
Darrin Lunde, Collections Manager, Department of
    Mammalogy, American Museum of Natural
    History, New York, NY

Printed in the United States

Photographic credits:
Front Cover: Nature PL: Anup Shah
Corbis: Bojan Brecelj 19r; **FLPA:** David Hosking
22tr, Frans Lanting 10r, Claus Meyer/Minden
Pictures 24, 28, Mark Newman 27b, Cyril Ruoso/JH
Editorial 14, 15br, Jurgen & Christine Sohns 16;
Nature PL: Ingo Arndt 4, 8, 9b, 18, Anup Shah 5b,
7l, 7r, 10l, Solvin Zankl 17t, Jean-Pierre
Zwaenepoel 20; **NHPA:** Kevin Schafer 26;
Photolibrary.com: Konrad Wothe 3, 12;
Shutterstock: Holger Ehlers 22br, 31, Nick Lamb
15bl, Yury Zaporozhchenko 13t; **Still Pictures:**
Doug Cheeseman 22, Cyril Ruoso/BIOS 21tl.

Contents

Any words that appear in the
text in bold, **like this**, are
explained in the glossary.

What Are Apes and Monkeys?

*Apes and monkeys are our closest animal relations. Like us, apes and monkeys are **mammals**. They have furry bodies and they feed their young with milk.*

The group of mammals that apes, monkeys, and humans belong to is called **primates**. Primates have a large brain and are usually **social** animals. Apes have no tail, and their arms are longer than their legs. Gorillas and chimpanzees are apes. Monkeys do have a tail. Macaques and baboons are monkeys.

All primates have a large, round head with a flattened face and forward facing eyes. Primates have a short nose, so their sense of smell is not as strong as that of many other animals. However, they can see and hear very well.

Primate Hands and Feet

The hands and feet of primates suit their different lifestyles. For example, the orangutan has a grasping big toe for climbing trees. The baboon has a slim foot for walking on the ground.

Gorilla hand

Orangutan foot

Macaque hand

Baboon foot

UP CLOSE

There are two kinds of monkeys: Old World monkeys and New World monkeys. New World monkeys live in Mexico, Central America, and South America. Most monkeys live in trees. Some can grip branches with their tail.

Orangutan

The orangutan is the largest of the tree living animals. These apes are found only on two Asian islands, Borneo and Sumatra.

There are two kinds of orangutans. One lives in the **swamps** of Borneo, and the other lives in the **rainforests** of Sumatra. They both have long, reddish fur. Orangutans prefer to live alone, rather than in **social** groups. They have a big brain, which means they are clever. Captured orangutans have even been taught how to **communicate** with humans by using sign language.

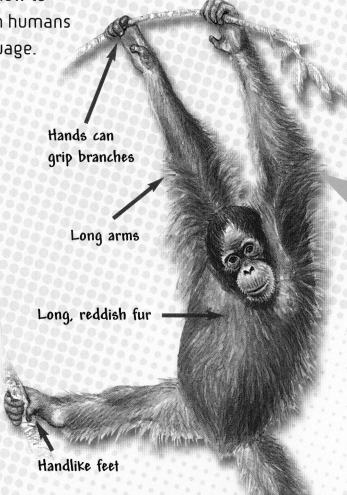

Hands can grip branches

Long arms

Long, reddish fur

Handlike feet

FACT FILE

Common name: orangutan
Scientific name: *Pongo pygmaeus* (Bornean) *Pongo abelii* (Sumatran)
Length: male up to 37 in (95 cm), female 29.5 in (75 cm)
Key features: very long arms, long fur, handlike feet
Diet: fruit, bark, insects

Orangutans in Danger

Orangutans are in danger because the trees in which they live are being cut down by people. People build houses or plant **crops** in place of the trees. Humans have also taken too many orangutans to live in zoos.

An orangutan mother carries her baby with her wherever she goes for the first two years of its life. She carries the baby against her chest until it is strong enough to ride on her back.

UP CLOSE

These long-armed apes are suited to forest living. Their arms are incredibly strong. Their fingers grip tightly, too. This means they can easily swing from one tree to another.

Mountain Gorilla

These gentle giants may look fierce, but they are not nearly as scary as they look. Mountain gorillas are generally shy animals. They prefer peace, quiet, and a long rest to fighting.

The gorilla's large body is covered in black fur. Males have some silver fur on their back. This gives them their name, silverbacks. Gorillas are **social** animals. A male leads a group of up to 40 gorillas. He fathers all the babies. The gorillas in the group like to **groom** each other, or clean each other's fur. Gorilla mothers look after their babies until they are four or five years old.

This is a silverback. The large patch of silver fur on its back shows it is a fully grown male and the leader of the group.

UP CLOSE

Gorillas are huge! Females weigh twice as much as a fully grown person. Males weigh four times as much. Gorillas walk on all fours, resting on the **knuckle pads** on their hands.

FACT FILE

Common name: mountain gorilla
Scientific name: *Gorilla beringei beringei*
Height: males 4.6–5.9 ft (1.4–1.8 m), females 4.3–5 ft (1.3–1.5 m)
Key features: large, barrel-shaped body, black fur, broad face
Diet: leaves, berries, and bark

Large barrel-shaped body

No tail

Legs shorter than arms

Large, wide face

Long, muscular arms

Protective Giant

After eating at midday, all the gorillas in a group gather around the male silverback. The male protects the females and the young gorillas.

The silverback is at the front of this group.

Chimpanzee

The chimpanzee is one of our closest relatives. This clever animal forms strong friendships with other chimpanzees. They even call upon their friends to help them in a fight!

Chimpanzees live in large groups. A group can include up to 120 animals, but the chimpanzees do not live together all the time. They break into smaller groups for different activities. While one large group searches for birds' eggs, another smaller group might look for berries and insects. Female chimpanzees look after the young and one male leads the group. The other males sometimes join together to challenge the leader.

Chimpanzees use **tools**, such as leaves, to clean themselves or pick up prickly fruit. This clever chimpanzee is using a stick to clean its teeth.

Bonobos

Bonobos are very like chimpanzees, but they are slimmer and have longer legs. They also have a black face. They live in groups in central Africa. Bonobos are even more closely related to us than chimpanzees.

Bonobos have pink lips and long black hair on their heads.

Making
a threat

Fear or
excitement

Play face

UP CLOSE

Chimpanzees **communicate** with each other by hugging, kissing, **grooming**, and patting. They also pull many different faces to show what they are thinking.

Asking
for food

FACT FILE

Common name: chimpanzee
Scientific name: *Pan troglodytes*
Length: head and body of males 27.5–35 in (70–89 cm), females 25–33 in (63–84 cm)
Key features: brownish black fur, a bare face, which is brownish pink
Diet: fruit, flowers, bark, insects, birds' eggs, meat

Japanese Macaque

This woolly animal is also known as a snow monkey. It lives in the mountains of Japan, where it is very cold. The monkey needs a thick, woolly coat to keep warm. Its red face and bottom certainly stand out in the snow!

The Japanese macaque lives in highland forests. It likes to eat fruit, berries, flowers, and leaves. Sometimes it eats small animals. These monkeys live in large groups called **troops.** A male leads the troop. When the group travels, the monkeys follow each other in a row. The most important male guards the females and the young as they travel.

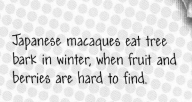

Japanese macaques eat tree bark in winter, when fruit and berries are hard to find.

Taking a Bath

These monkeys often keep warm in winter by sitting in hot spring water. The whole troop sits peacefully together. The animals **groom** each other while they bathe.

These macaques are grooming each other.

FACT FILE

Common name: Japanese macaque
Scientific name: Macaca fuscata
Length: head and body of males 18.5–24 in (47–60cm), females 15.5–26.5 in (7–12 cm)
Key features: thick, brown coat in winter, bare, red face and bottom, short tail
Diet: fruit, berries, flowers and leaves, insects, and small animals

Red face

Thick, woolly fur

UP CLOSE

In summer, Japanese macaques lose their thick fur coat. The coat grows back again in time for the freezing winter. The monkeys also eat more in summer. That helps them to build up fat to survive the winter.

Barbary Macaque

The barbary macaque is the only African macaque. It is difficult to see its tiny tail, so people often think it is an ape. Barbary macaques live in the forests of North America.

Barbary macaques are in danger because people are cutting down the forests to grow **crops**. That forces the macaques to move to higher ground, where there is less food. Sometimes they take their revenge by stealing people's crops! Female barbary macaques have just one baby at a time. This is why it takes a long time for the number of macaques to increase.

Precious Babies

Female barbary macaques cannot have babies until they are four years old. They look after their young for a whole year. The males help with the childcare, too.

A female with a baby and young macaque.

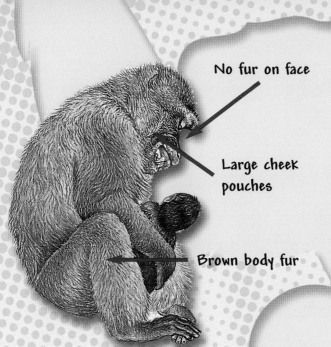

No fur on face

Large cheek pouches

Brown body fur

FACT FILE

Common name: barbary macaque
Scientific name: *Macaca sylvanus*
Length: head and body up to 22–30 in (55–76 cm)
Key features: very small tail, bare face with large cheek pouches
Diet: mostly plants, some insects, especially caterpillars

UP CLOSE

A group of about 100 barbary macaques live wild on the Rock of Gibraltar, in the Mediterranean, off the coast of Spain. Barbary macaques are the only monkey to still live in the wild in Europe.

Male barbary macaques will never attack a baby. Males often hold a baby to stop another male attacking them.

Black Macaque

*You can tell a black macaque by the crest of hair on the top of its head. Black macaques live in large groups in the **rainforests** of Sulawesi, Indonesia.*

Black macaques have a long, narrow, black face. They are black all over, apart from their pink bottom. They live in **troops** of up to 100 animals. Members of the troop **groom** each other to strengthen the bond between them. They are less **aggressive** than other kinds of macaque. They spend a lot of time searching for food in the rainforest.

Black macaques spend a lot of time grooming each other.

UP CLOSE

Black macaques make loud screams to stop troop members fighting. They also scream to scare away another troop. Black macaques talk by making faces. These include smacking their lips and staring with an open mouth.

Crest of black hair on top of head

Long, black face

Black fur

Small tail

FACT FILE

Common name: black macaque
Scientific name: *Macaca nigra*
Length: head and body of males 20–22 in (51–56 cm), females 18–20 in (46–51 cm)
Key features: long and thin black face, large cheek pouches, pink bottom, very small tail
Diet: fruit, leaves, birds' eggs, sometimes **crops**

Storing Food

Black macaques can store food in large pouches in their cheeks. They eat the food later, when it is safe to stop and chew it! They mostly look for food in the trees.

Hamadryas Baboon

These baboons live in small groups that are ruled by one male. Each male ruler keeps his group under tight control, and uses force to stop anyone stepping out of line!

Male hamadryas baboons have a long, silver-gray coat. Each male lives in a small group, with about five females and their young. These small groups join together to form bigger groups. These large groups then travel and look for food together. At night they join other large groups, to make even bigger **troops**. The baboons sleep together in these large troops. When a young male becomes an adult, he leaves the troop to start up his own small group.

Hamadryas baboons spend much of their day **grooming** each other.

Sacred Monkey

The hamadryas baboon was a **sacred**, or **holy**, animal in ancient Egypt. Carvings of it have been found on temples. Hamadryas baboons no longer live in Egypt.

An ancient Egyptian baboon wall painting.

No fur on face

Thick, gray fur around head

Red bottom

Long tail

FACT FILE

Common name: hamadryas baboon
Scientific name: *Papio hamadryas hamadryas*
Length: head and body of males 27.5–37 in (70–95 cm), females 20–25.5 in (50–65 cm)
Key features: bare, red face, long fur, males have thicker fur on shoulders
Diet: grass, fruit, insects, hares

UP CLOSE

Male hamadryas baboons have a magnificent, thick collar of fur around their neck.

Hanuman Langur

These long-tailed monkeys are a common sight in India. They live in forests, dry areas, mountains, and even villages and towns!

Hanuman langurs have a slender body and a black face. They have a large **brow**. Hanuman langurs are peaceful, gentle animals. A male leads a group for about three years, then a younger male takes over. These monkeys mainly eat leaves. They need to eat a lot of leaves to get enough **nourishment**. Hanuman langurs may have to travel over a large area to find enough food to eat.

These hanuman langurs are sitting on a roof in an Indian town.

UP CLOSE

The young males in a **troop** play games together. They also fight. This prepares them for when they grow up and lead their own troops.

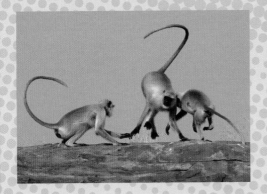

FACT FILE

Common name: hanuman langur
Scientific name: Semnopithecus entellus
Length: head and body 16–31 in (41–78 cm)
Key features: slender with a long tail, black face, large brow
Diet: leaves, some fruit and flowers, and sometimes crops

Black face

Brown body fur

White fur around face

Hindu Monkey-God

Hanuman langurs are named after the Hindu monkey-god. They are thought to be **sacred**, or **holy**, in India. They are even allowed to steal **crops**.

Black hands and feet

Long tail

Black and White Colobus Monkey

This monkey from central Africa has thick, black fur and a long cape of white hair. It also has furry, white cheeks!

Black and white colobus monkeys can eat old leaves and plants. So they can live in dry areas and mountains, as well as lush **rainforest**. They live in small groups, which consist of one male with up to six females and their young. A baby may be looked after by a female who is not its mother. Colobus monkeys are very friendly. They **groom**, comb, and stroke each other.

UP CLOSE

Each morning, at dawn, colobus monkeys start a loud chorus of croaking and roaring in the trees. They also jump about in the trees and shake their long, white cape. This lets other colobus monkeys know they are there!

Clever Coloring

Their long, white cape makes colobus monkeys look much bigger than they are. They also have bushy, white hair at the end of their tail.

Black and white colobus monkeys spend most of their day high up in the trees.

Bushy tail

White fur cape

White fur on face

FACT FILE

Common name: black and white colobus monkey
Scientific name: *Colobus guereza*
Length: head and body 2–26 in (50–66 cm)
Key features: white cape of fur and long white fur on the end of the tail, black body
Diet: mostly leaves, also fruit and seeds

Brown Howler Monkey

This monkey lives in the forests of Brazil. It likes to shout loudly from the treetops every morning! Its deafening chorus can be heard from a long way off.

Brown howler monkeys are dark, reddish brown in color. The throat of the male looks swollen because of its large, bony **"voice box."** It uses its voice box to make loud howls and roars. Howler monkeys live in the trees almost all the time. They search for the juiciest leaves, ripe fruits, and flowers. They also spend at least half the day resting.

Howler monkeys live high up in trees, where they are safe from **predators**.

Males have a swollen
throat for howling

Reddish brown fur

Living to Old Age

Brown howler monkeys can live for about 15 years. That is longer than many other monkeys.

Long tail can grip branches

UP CLOSE

Howler monkeys have a very long **prehensile** tail. This means the tail can grip. They use it to grip branches as they leap from tree to tree.

FACT FILE

Common name: brown howler monkey
Scientific name: *Alouatta fusca*
Length: head and body 18–23 in (45–58 cm)
Key features: chubby, with a long, furry tail, males have a swollen throat
Diet: mainly leaves, some fruit

Black-Handed Spider Monkey

These monkeys love trees! They live in leafy forests, where they walk along the treetops. Black-handed spider monkeys can also swing gracefully from branch to branch.

Black-handed spider monkeys use their hands to pick fruit from the trees in the forests of Central America. They also eat flowers, nuts, and sometimes birds' eggs, too. They live in groups of about 20 monkeys. More monkeys will gather at a tree full of ripe fruit, such as mangoes. Females have just one baby at a time. Black-handed spider monkeys live for up to 20 years in the wild.

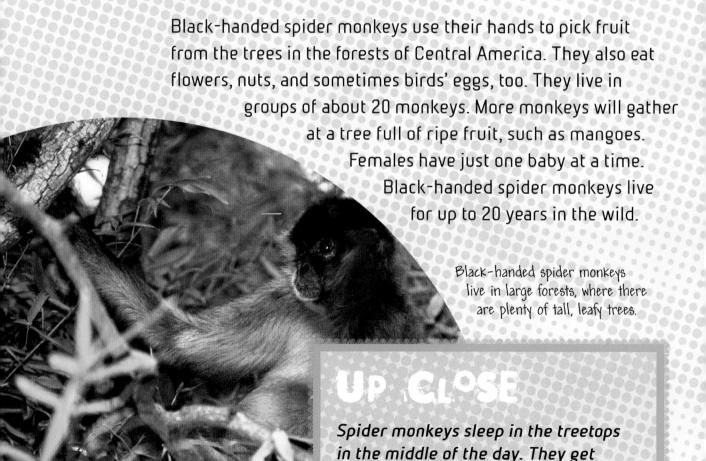

Black-handed spider monkeys live in large forests, where there are plenty of tall, leafy trees.

UP CLOSE

Spider monkeys sleep in the treetops in the middle of the day. They get cross if they are disturbed. They stamp or throw branches at any intruders!

FACT FILE

Common name: black-handed spider monkey
Scientific name: Ateles geoffroyi
Length: head and body 13–20 in (34–52 cm)
Key features: short, thin brown fur, black hands and feet, long arms, legs, and tail
Diet: leaves and fruit, sometimes birds' eggs

Long, spiderlike arms and legs

Long, strong tail can grip branches

Black hands and feet

Like a Spider

The long arms, legs, and tail of the spider monkey give it its name. It looks like a spider! The spider monkey uses its long **limbs** and tail to swing through the trees. It can even hang by its **prehensile** tail!

Spider monkeys grip the branches of trees with their hands and feet.

27

Woolly Monkey

This stocky creature is one of the largest monkeys in South America. It is called a woolly monkey because its fur is so woolly.

The **rainforest** is home for the woolly monkey. It lives up in the treetops, where it looks for ripe fruit. It rarely comes down to the ground. This monkey's thick coat varies in color from blue-gray to brown or black. Sometimes, woolly monkeys mix with other monkeys, such as howler monkeys. They can look out for danger together. These monkeys are at risk from people, who catch the babies to sell as pets.

This woolly monkey is gripping a tree branch with its tail.

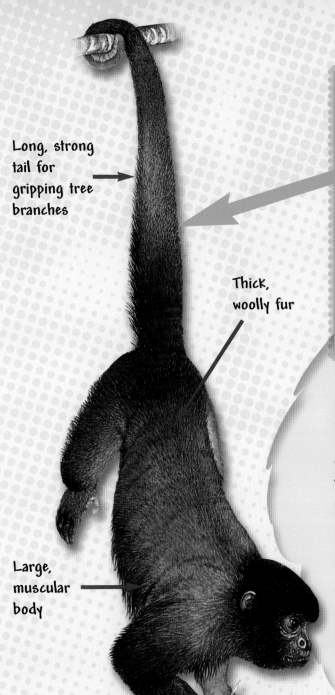

Long, strong tail for gripping tree branches

Thick, woolly fur

Large, muscular body

FACT FILE

Common name: woolly monkey
Scientific name: *Lagothrix lagotricha*
Length: head and body 18–25.5 in (46–65 cm)
Key features: thick fur, a rounded head, and a strong tail
Diet: fruit, some plants

Marking Territory

Male woolly monkeys mark their **territory** to warn off other males. They wet a surface with their spit, then rub their chest on it to leave their **scent** behind.

Glossary

brow The forehead of an animal or person.

communicate To 'talk' using either speech or body language.

crop A large number of plants grown for food.

groom To clean the fur of another animal.

holy Pure and godlike.

knuckle pad A soft pad that protects the bony part of a finger.

limb An arm or leg.

mammal A warm-blooded animal that feeds its babies with milk.

nourishment The energy and vitamins and minerals found in food.

predator An animal that hunts other animals for food.

prehensile To be able to grip something.

primate One of a group of mammals that includes monkeys and apes.

rainforest A thick forest in a warm area where a lot of rain falls.

sacred Something that is protected because it is thought to be holy.

scent The special smell an animal makes, often to mark its territory.

social Friendly.

swamp An area of very wet ground.

territory An area of land in which an animal lives.

tool Something used to make an activity easier, such as digging the ground to find food.

troop A group of monkeys.

voice box Part of the body, found in the throat, through which sounds are made.

Further Resources

Books about apes and monkeys

Animals in Danger: Mountain Gorilla by Rod Theodorou,
　Heinemann Library, 2001

Gorillas by Seymour Simon, HarperTrophy, 2003

Our Wild World: Chimpanzees by Deborah Dennard, Northword Press, 2003

Watching Orangutans in Asia by Deborah Underwood,
　Heinemann Library, 2006

Wildlife Survival: Orangutans in Danger by Helen Orme,
　Bearport Publishing, 2006

Zoobooks: Apes by John Bonnett Wexo, Wildlife Education, 2001

Useful websites

http://kids.nationalgeographic.com/Animals/CreatureFeature/

http://www.cambodianwildliferescue.org/

http://www.cercopan.org/

http://www.chunkymonkey.com/murals/
　　gibbonlesson.htm

http://www.congogorillaforest.com/
　　congohome

Index